SCOTTISH FISHING BOATS
A NEW LOOK

JAMES A. POTTINGER

The
History
Press

A later major conversion saw the *Sustain* PD108 with a full shelterdeck and rigged for pair seining. She was decommissioned and broken up at Peterhead.

First published 2009

Reprinted 2010

The History Press
The Mill, Brimscombe Port
Stroud, Gloucestershire, GL5 2QG
www.thehistorypress.co.uk

British Library Cataloguing in Publication Data.
A catalogue record for this book is available from the British Library.

ISBN 978 0 7524 5304 0

Typesetting and origination by The History Press
Printed in Great Britain

SCOTTISH FISHING BOATS
A NEW LOOK

Radiant Star LK71.

CONTENTS

ACKNOWLEDGEMENTS

Back in 2005 my book *Fishing Boats of Scotland* was published, and I am gratified that it has proved popular with a wide circle of readers interested in the various types of boats I illustrated.

Hopefully this volume will be of similar interest, the result of a trawl through the ever-growing collection of photos I have taken over many years. Given the movements and decommissioning of boats in the interim before publication, some information could well be out of date. I have widened the scope somewhat on this occasion to include some smaller craft and boats not from Scotland, which nevertheless have often appeared in northern waters.

Much of the information relating to the history of many of the boats shown here has been gleaned from the pages of the invaluable annual *Fishing Vessels of Britain & Ireland*, compiled by David Linkie, and the weekly issues of *Fishing News*, not to forget the informative and illustrated books by Gloria Wilson, and the definitive volume *Purse Seiners* by Sam Henderson and Peter Drummond, who have also provided additional data on many boats.

To all of the above, I gratefully acknowledge their help.

INTRODUCTION

The reduction of the Scottish fleet in the wake of various measures under the guise of conservation and other restrictions has had an equally negative impact on the landward side of the industry. Furthermore, the trend to ever greater centralisation means that many of the smaller ports around our coastline present but a shadow of the activity previously enjoyed there. It is now noticeable that some of these harbours, formerly busy with big fishing boats, are now home to a large fleet of angling boats which attract amateur fishermen often from a long distance away.

The cycle of highs and lows ever associated with the fishing industry is still with us; the uncertainty from one year to the next with respect to quotas make it very difficult to plan for the future, but, as I write, the seine net and trawl fleets are enjoying a welcome boost in landing prices to offset the ever higher fuel costs, and it is gratifying to see that a number of new boats are either entering or about to enter service.

A feature of the changes in the industry has been the increase in the number of small boats engaged in catching various types of shellfish, some of them conversions of older craft but many more new purpose-built boats with a high degree of sophistication applied to gear and electronics. Some smaller inshore shellfish boats also make an entry. In this class of boat, twin-hulled catamarans are gradually gaining popularity despite some initial scepticism, primarily due to their stability and increased deck area, which is of particular advantage when handling crab pots and creels.

The heavy displacement of the powerful steel fishing boat of today is a safer and much more efficient unit, with a whole host of labour-saving devices which could only be dreamed about by the fishermen of yesteryear.

Even with these advances the working deck of a modern fishing boat is no place for the fainthearted, but when comparing the amount of manual labour involved on the exposed fore decks of former distant and middle-water trawlers the comparison is stark indeed.

On the negative side it has to be admitted that the modern fishing boats lack the grace of the cruiser-sterned wooden boats of the 1950s and '60s, the years inevitably taking their toll on the numbers of these handsome boats.

The broad descriptions of the various types outlined in my earlier book, *Fishing Boats of Scotland*, are still valid, and to avoid repetition these have not been included here. The subsequent selection of pictures follow in no particular order.

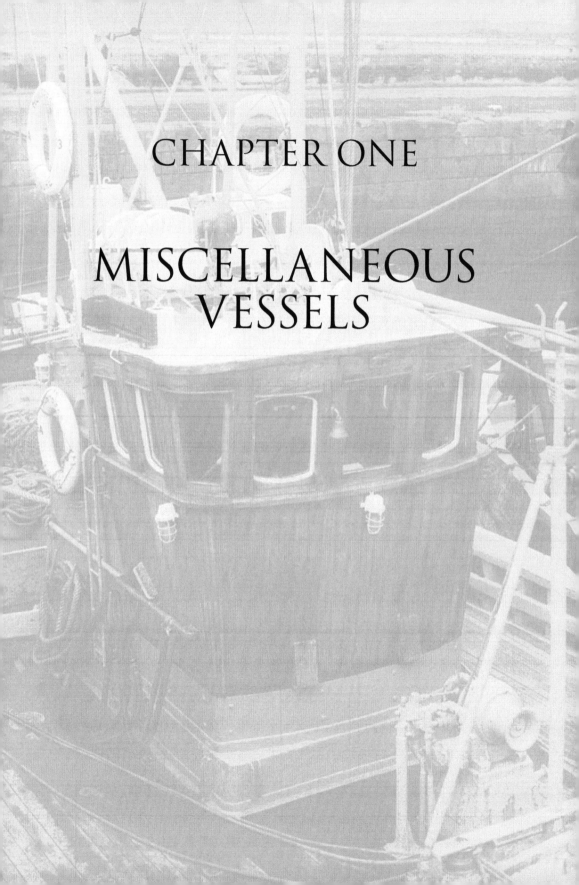

CHAPTER ONE

MISCELLANEOUS VESSELS

Sunbeam LK335. Designed by the Aberdeen naval architects Johnson & Smart, she was built by the Zamakona Yard in Spain in 1997. She was sold to Faeroe in 2007, a victim of EU quota cuts and the reduction of deepwater opportunities. Previously catching as much as 300 tons in two months, fishing in waters as deep as 850 fathoms around Rockall, the last deepwater quota was reduced to 30 tons.

Mizpah BF57. Built by Thomson's Yard at Buckie, she was the first boat in Britain to fit the Spanish Aka power block, manufactured by the firm Ibercisca of Vigo.

Bracoden BF37 was the first in a trio of sister vessels built by Hugh McLean at Renfrew in 1970, and the fourth since they branched out into fishing boat construction.

Designed as a seiner trawler with an overall length of 82ft 6in, accommodation was provided for eight crewmembers, and, unusually, she had a cabin fitted with two berths aft of the wheelhouse for WFA or HIB technicians and scientists. She was renamed *Brighter Morn* BF 818 before being sold to Kilkeel in 1999.

Illustrious PD27. Seen here being stripped, she was built at Skaalurens Skipsbyggeri at Rosendal in Norway in 1949. She was bought by a Shetland partnership in 1967 and renamed *Adalla* LK719, fishing with a Peterhead skipper. Initially successful at pursing, she was then beset with problems and laid up at Peterhead in 1968, finally being converted under new owners for seine netting and renamed *Illustrious* in 1972.

Laid up in 1981, she suffered a fire after which she was stripped of all working gear then set alight in Peterhead Harbour, her remains being broken up on the beach.

Aeolus BCK143. Unusually among fishing boats she was painted white, setting off her handsome lines. Built by the Macduff Boatbuilding & Engineering Co. in 1977 to a G.L. Watson design, her name represents the God of the Winds in Greek mythology.

Ardelle BCK227. Built by Herd & MacKenzie at Buckie in 1964 with a Mercedes engine, which was later replaced with a Kelvin, she is seen here before being extensively altered with a raised wheelhouse and shelterdeck, which completely transformed her appearance. She was decommissioned in 2002.

Eclipse PD38. This 80ft-long powerful boat was built by Forbes at Sandhaven as *Kallista* FR107 in 1972, one of the last boats designed by Roderick Forbes. She was later renamed *Sharon Dawn* before taking the name *Eclipse*, under which she was lost by sinking after catching on fire 120 miles north-east of Peterhead in September 1989. With a massive 850bhp Caterpillar engine she could do 14 knots, and was intended to fish on the more distant grounds.

Dalma BCK113. Another boat which had her appearance transformed with the addition of whaleback and shelterdeck.

Celerity LK 187. The first cruiser-sterned boat built by Herd & MacKenzie at Buckie was completed in 1933 as Yard No.43. The BCK 142 was a 56ft boat with 54bhp Gardner engine. Sold to Shetland, she took the number LK187 and was later fitted with a new wheelhouse, before moving to South Shields in around 1973. Finally she moved to Holland where she was converted into a motor yacht.

Celerity. When living in Holland from 1985–89 I was amazed to see a bow I recognised jutting out among all the traditional Dutch craft and modern yachts at Vlaardingen. This indeed proved to be the former fishing boat *Celerity,* with the fish hold now converted to a saloon, and I was able to talk to the owner who was naturally surprised to meet anyone who recognised her from the past.

Derona A242. Whilst the main building yards were situated at Macduff, Fraserburgh, Buckie and Sandhaven, Jones of Buckie also operated a yard and slipway at Lossiemouth. One of the last boats to be built there was the 54ft *Derona* for an Aberdeen skipper of the Don Fishing Co. She was later renamed *Emulous II* FR43. She later sank WNW of Cape Wrath on 23 January 1995.

Deejay BF257. Built by the Macduff Boat Building & Engineering Co. Ltd in 1977 for Fleetwood owners who operated in the Irish Sea, she was later converted for scallop fishing, as seen in this photo, and then bought by an Arbroath skipper who added a shelterdeck.

Forth Ranger KY20. This 40ft wooden boat was built in 1974 by Robsons of South Shields, and was perhaps unique in that she had a steel transom grafted on to her original cruiser stern. This was done by attaching brackets to the hull, aft on which was welded a 3/16in-thick steel plate. The inner space was then filled with polystyrene and polyurethane foam to seal the space completely. Rebuilt in 2004, her transom was removed and converted to a crabber, operating from Wicklow.

Forth Ranger KY20, shown with her added steel transom.

Evangeline. On the slip at St Monans after being converted to a yacht, this boat was built as long ago as 1920, at Fraserburgh, and numbered FR163. She went to Shetland in 1967 to Scalloway owners. She left the islands in the mid-1970s and is listed in the 1980 Olsens Almanac as DE26.

Illustrious BF438. Built by George Thomson at Buckie in 1966 as a 69ft seiner, later moving to Fraserburgh in 1984 and being renamed *Chrisannryl* FR346. Converted to trawling, she was renamed *Golden Ray* by a Buckie skipper, but was sold to Portavogie in 1994. Decommissioned in 2004, she has now been replaced by a new *Golden Ray* B963, built by John Kearney of Kilkeel as the first new-build to the Northern Irish port of Portavogie in sixteen years.

Mia Jane W FR443 was built in France in 1990 as the *Nicholas Jereon*, then fished from Castletownbere in Ireland under the name *Boy Jason* S41 in 2000. Later renamed *Ocean Reaper II*, in 2003 she was bought by the former owners of the *Steadfast* FR443, a boat which was shown going to the breakers in the TV documentary *Gutted*. She is the first Fraserburgh-owned French-built trawler.

Westward PD345. Built by Richard Irvin & Sons at Peterhead in 1960 as *Fragrance* PD345 and designed for herring drift netting, seine netting and great line fishing. She was one of the last boats to use herring drift nets, and the first to have the more powerful Kelvin 249bhp diesel fitted. This photograph shows her lying alongside the *Illustrious* PD27 being stripped.

Ocean Dawn KY371. Completed in 1956 by Richards Shipbuilders at Lowestoft as YH77 for Bloomfields Ltd, this steel drifter trawler came north to Scotland in 1969 and operated as a line fishing boat under the registration number KY371. She was caught under the piers at Aberdeen on 10 September 1979 and sank, but was later raised. In 1984 she was converted to a standby safety vessel and renamed *Rewga*, but then in 1987 was sold to Sweden, re-taking her former name. She came back to the UK in 1998 and is now a houseboat on the south coast.

Olive Leaf BCK210. Completed at St Monans in 1948 and looking well kept and neat at Lochinver, I saw her next lying at Fairlie Marina on the Clyde in 2007, converted to a motor yacht. As she has been there a few years now it is not certain if she will be launched again.

Quiet Waters III FR353. Ready for launching by the Macduff Boatbuilding & Engineering Co. in 1980 as a dual-purpose pelagic and whitefish pair trawler, she was fitted with RSW tanks. Her varnished hull shows the true skill of the boatbuilder who used wood. She went to Portavogie in 1995 as B221 where her RSW tanks were removed, and she was used for semi-pelagic whitefish trawling. In 2007 she was sold to Shetland owners.

Silver Gem INS61. Built by James Noble at Fraserburgh in 1972 as a seiner and ring netter, INS61 went to an Avoch skipper before moving to Campbeltown and taking the number CN297. Moving to Moray in the early 1980s, she was extensively modernised and in 1985 took the number BF27 and a new skipper/owner. She was replaced by the new *Antaries* BF27, completed by Buckie Shipyard in 2001, after which she was sold and renamed *Ocean Wanderer* FR946, being decommissioned in 2002.

Kelly BCK303. Built by Herd & MacKenzie at Buckie in 1982 as a gill netter for Danbrit of Grimsby, she was later converted to a whitefish trawler after being sold to Locker Trawlers of Whitby. Converted for scallop dredging by Macduff Shipyards in 1994, she is fishing now under the number DS 7.

Smallwood BCK27. Built in 1966 by the Ramsey Shipbuilding & Engineering Co. in the Isle of Man, this small steel trawler was a regular visitor to Aberdeen, in which port she is seen leaving on a bright day. Portable boards have been shipped along the bulwark to give some added protection, the 'French' flag indicating that she is pairing.

Star of Bethlehem PD96. Built by Herd & MacKenzie in 1968 as the *Ajax* INS168, after being sold to Peterhead she was renamed *Harvest Hope* in 1973, *Star of Bethlehem* in 1976, *Opportunus* in 1987 and finally *Benaiah III* N841 in 1995.

White Heather IV LH1. This boat was the first of a new class of seiners/trawlers built by the Eyemouth Boat Building Co. in 1968 and commissioned by Jim Aitchison. She is one of six *White Heathers* owned by the family. At 51ft long she had a forward engine room and coiled her seine net warps forward at each side of the wheelhouse. A prolific fisher, as the third smallest boat in the fleet she set a record at Eyemouth in 1973 for 200 days' fishing when she grossed £114,000. Later registered as OB266, she was based at Mallaig and was still fishing in 2007.

Dauntless II LK531. Arriving in Shetland in March 1961 as *Dauntless II*, she was a 75ft boat built by J. & G. Forbes at Sandhaven, and the first in Shetland to be fitted with a chilled hold. She is seen here lying at her homeport of Hamnavoe Burra Isle. On 7 March 1963 she found a depth charge in her net when fishing off Burra. Later fitted with a whaleback and enclosed shelterdeck, she was sold to Buckie owners in 1988 and renamed *Choice* BCK200.

Choice BCK200 is seen here leaving Buckie. After leaving fishing, she was bought by Nitro Classic in 1997, intended to be used for marketing purposes, and underwent a twelve-month refit at Gloucester to equip her for corporate 'team building' courses. On one such trip, sailing from London to Antwerp, she went aground on Blyth Sands River Thames Sea Reach at 06.40 on 9 August 2001. She was later relocated at 13.33 with only superficial damage.

Star of Peace PD324. The fine lines and altogether slender shape indicate a design of an earlier era, having been completed in 1961 by Irvin at Peterhead. Readily identified by the sloping stepped front of her wheelhouse, in this instance she is being towed into Peterhead. She ended her days fishing from South Shields, and was broken up on a quay.

The 45ft *Sylvanus* was built in 1910 by Walter Duncan at Hamnavoe in Shetland on the traditional lines of a large sixern; fitted with a 25bhp Gardner engine, she was given the fishing number LK171. Used originally for line and summer herring fishing, as a seine netter she was one of the first boats in the seine net fleet to fit a warp coiler. She was later re-fitted with a diesel engine, and ended her days as a flit boat owned by the Shetland Council.

This is a later view of *Sylvanus* in July 1972 of her last resting place on Hay's slip at Scalloway, in the shadow of Scalloway Castle. Her graceful form is still evident from the shape of the frames now visible with the deck cut off.

The wooden cruiser-sterned *Comet* LK253, seen her on the Malakoff slip at Lerwick, was built at Flekkefjord in Norway for the Burra partners in 1971, ultimately being sold to Irish owners in 1990.

Rose of Sharon III LH56. Pictured coming in past Burra en route to Scalloway, she is one of the impressive boats with a three-quarter shelterdeck built by Forbes at Sandhaven in 1983 for Longniddry owners. On being sold to a Fraserburgh skipper to replace the *Graceful* FR147, she was renamed *Minerva* FR147 and fully shelterdecked. Her last name was *Provider* PD250, in 1999, before being decommissioned in 2002.

Illustrious PD27. The former purser *Adalla* after conversion to a seine netter.

Favour INS235. Built in 1963 by Herd & MacKenzie at Buckie as a 60ft seiner and ringer named *Falcon*, she was partnered with *Flourish II* INS123, and operated mostly on the west coast. She was renamed *Favour* in 1976, when she was replaced by the new Campbeltown 75ft *Falcon*. Decommissioned at Kilkeel in 1996.

Replenish FR199. A Richard Irvin boat built in 1975, she spent periods pair trawling for herring on the west coast. Later shelterdecked, she replaced the *Bounteous Sea* FR399 that had been built by Forbes at Sandhaven in 1969, and took her name in 1997. She was decommissioned in 2003/2004.

Achieve FR100. Built by Richard Irvin at Peterhead in 1972, she was later renamed *Complete*, but never fished as such. After decommissioning she was stripped down to deck level and underwent a major reconstruction to convert her into a private motor cruising yacht. Her former wheelhouse stands in the car park adjacent to the Satrosphere building at the bottom of Constitution Street in Aberdeen.

Helena FR178. This boat was built by J. & G. Forbes in 1975 as a whitefish and pelagic trawler. She had a fiery end when she went ablaze at Fraserburgh in March 2007. She was renamed *Crystal River* and *Westhaven*, and finally, as a twin-rigger, *Ocean Quest* FR375.

Janet Sate FR107. The *Coromandel* was built by James N. Miller at St Monans, and the sister vessel *Janet Sate* was subcontracted to J. & G. Forbes of Sandhaven and completed in 1984 for Riverside Trawlers of Grimsby, a Jens Bojen concern. Designed as a pair trawler only and intended to pair with the *Wendy Pulfrey*, she had a high freeboard and volume forward to ensure level trim when full of ice and a catch. Later renamed *Strathnairn* INS 185, *Alba* PD181 and *Carisanne II* FR107, she was fully shelterdecked and converted to a pair seiner.

A view of the crowded harbour at Peterhead, with the handsome *Transcend* BCK167 in the centre. Built by Forbes in 1966 as the herring boat *Diligence* FR391, she was renamed in 1978. She was sold to Wick in 1992 and registered as WK167. Her conversion to an offshore crabber in 1999 included a vivier tank, hauler and creel stowage. Unfortunately she caught on fire and was lost in February 2004.

The pioneering *Constellation* FR294 could claim to be the first transom seiner trawler built in Scotland when built by Forbes at Sandhaven in 1965. She had a forward wheelhouse, open aft deck and a net-shooting opening in the bulwark in the transom. She moved to Ireland in 1978 and was re-registered as *Constellation* C N293. She was decommissioned in 2002.

Sustain PD108. Still sporting the star on her exhaust casing, as when originally painted, she was built as the 76ft seiner and herring pair trawler *Sparkling Star*. Later she was renamed *Rosemount* and is now at Macduff awaiting conversion to a house boat.

Ocean Gem BA265. Built by A. Noble at Girvan in 1964, with sister *Pathfinder* BA252, both were sold when skippers built the purser *Pathfinder* BA188 in Norway. She operated as a ring netter and pair trawler. At one time she was varnished, then white, and latterly light blue. She alternated between herring pair trawling and ring netting, often working with *Britannia* BA267. Latterly a prawn trawl, she stopped fishing in 2006, and was possibly converted to a pleasure boat at Troon.

Fair Morn IV BA19. Built in 1973 at Macduff as *Athena* BF190, she then took the number CN262 in 1987 and INS 181 in 1988, and finally *Fair Morn IV* BA19 in 1991. She is shown here about to land at Troon on a blustery day in February 2005.

Respect BCK216. A product of George Thomson & Sons at Buckie in 1979, she was outfitted as a trawler with the ever popular Kelvin engine. She was registered as BF396 when sold to a Whitehills skipper who fished with her until taking delivery of the new *Prospect* BF573 from Macduff. Decommissioned in 2002.

Boy Andrew WK170. This Campbeltown 87ft cruiser-sterned seine net boat was completed in 1986, perpetuating the name of a series of previous boats.

Harvest Reaper BF214. Still fishing in 1983 with the rig of a typical early seine netter built in 1931 at Fraserburgh, the warps have been laid down on the side decks after being led off from the chain-driven coiler, and a powered roller is mounted aft to bring aboard the net, with tackle rigged on both sides of the aft mast to lift aboard the cod end. In later years she lay derelict on the pier at Burghead.

The 33ft *Gracious* FR167 was one of the beautifully shaped yoles built by Thomas Summers at Fraserburgh in the 1950s. Thomas Summers and partners set up their yard on the North Breakwater in 1948, having served their carpenter apprenticeships with James Noble. With no slipway, the boats were rolled along the quay to be launched at Nobles yard. For larger boats a temporary slipway frame was erected to ensure a more gentle baptism.

Built by Smith & Hutton at Anstruther in 1955 as the seiner drifter *Frigate* BCK26, and renamed *Jacana* BA138 after being sold to Ayrshire owners, she is seen here approaching the entrance channel to Girvan.

This cruiser-sterned boat is being framed at the Macduff boatyard. Note the substantial supports and posts to hold the frames in position at this early stage of construction.

View of two cruiser-sterned boats being built in the open at Macduff. Most likely the steam is from the steam box used to soften the various timbers to help in bending them around the hull.

Starella PD112. Completed in 1970 as a 78ft overall multi-purpose boat capable of seining or trawling, she was at that time the largest boat built by the Macduff Boatbuilding & Engineering Co. Ltd. She joined the 'PD' registered *Achilles*, with which she pair trawled for herring, as the second yellow-painted boat in the Peterhead fleet. Of larch planking on oak frames, she had a steel whaleback and deckhouse, in contrast to the now universal use of aluminium.

Edelweiss FR104. Completed in 1972 by James Noble at Fraserburgh, this trawler moved to the west coast and took the number SY337.

Rowanlea A832. Built in 1963 as *Welsh Prince*, and one of four sisters built at Newport, Monmouth, she worked out of Aberdeen under the BUT flag before being sold to Spain.

Ardent FR266. Built by John Lewis at Aberdeen in 1972 as seine netter *Seringa* PD95. Later she was renamed *Headway* PD346, *Julie Ann* FR122 and latterly *Ardent* FR266, before being decommissioned in 2002.

Comrades LK325. Lying in idyllic surroundings at Hamnavoe Pier on Burra Isle, she is the last of the older type of dual-purpose boats working the seine net on the inshore grounds, mostly fishing in the Burra Haaf, landing her catch at Scalloway and overnighting at her homeport. This 53ft boat was built by John Watt at Banff in 1958, and formerly followed the traditional routine of seine netting in winter months and herring drift netting in early summer and autumn at home in East Anglia.

Strathyre FR4. This lovely looking boat was built by James Noble at Fraserburgh in 1968. In 1995 she had the name *Freedom* CN194, and was last seen (2008) laid up at Peterhead in a dilapidated condition.

Julie Anne BCK140. She was completed as a 74ft seine netter by Herd & MacKenzie at Buckie for a local skipper in 1977. In 1983 she moved to Fraserburgh and re-registered as *Three Sisters* FR96 before being converted for trawling and crossing to Mallaig where she fished until being decommissioned in 2002.

Sedulous IV KY277. As one of the biggest wooden boats built at St Monans by James N. Miller Ltd, this seiner had white masts and spars and her hull was painted light blue before a black colour was applied to the hull along with buff to the masts. Her white wheelhouse, positioned well aft near the stern, was later grained. She had a soft-nosed stern, as on many Miller boats. She was decommissioned in 2002.

Salamis PD142. A development of the original Spinningdale design, and designated as MkII, she was completed by John Lewis in 1974 as a seiner trawler. At one time she also pair trawled for herring. She later took the name *Harvest Reaper* PD142, but was renamed *Shalimar* PD303 in1996. She was decommissioned in 2002.

St Kilda INS 47. Built by Herd & MacKenzie in 1978, and designed for the deep waters off the west coast, she fished very successfully out of Lochinver for many years. Replaced by the Macduff-built *Westro* INS20 in 1992, she was sold and renamed *Qui Vive* FR201 and operated as a twin-rig trawler with an extended shelterdeck. A change of name took place in 1998, when renamed *Dalriada* BF262, before being decommissioned in 2002 and scrapped at Denmark.

Borgoygutt N342. Completed by the Mandal Slipp & Mek. Verksted at Mandal in 1975, acquired by Richard Donnan in 1979 and registered at Newry, at 180.77ft overall length she was the largest boat in the N.I. fleet. The changing economics of the pelagic fisheries and difficulties in finding suitable crew saw her sale back to Norway and take the name *Radek* (II) H-22-A, then brought back to the UK by the Tait family in 1986 and renamed *Philorth* FR228, then sold to Faeroe in 2002 as *Nordbugvin* TN30.

Courage BF212 (I). One of the rare UK-built pursers, completed in 1974 at yard number 965 by Hall Russell in Aberdeen. Originally 88.3ft long, she was lengthened twice, by 19.37ft and 16.05ft, her open decks being shelterdecked with a new wheelhouse and whaleback being added at Holland during her career. She was sold in 1996 to be replaced by *Azalea* (2) and renamed *Fairy* H-12-B of Haugseund, and later *Veronica* GG522 and *Veronica av Foto* GG812 of Foto Sweden.

Lunar Bow (2) PD265. Seen on a fresh day in June 1986 leaving Aberdeen is another Sigbjorn Iversen product, completed in 1978 for the Buchan family of Peterhead, and used both as a purser and whitefisher. She was lengthened by 19.5ft in 1979 and then again by 6.61ft in 1983. Sold and renamed in 1987 as *Westward* BF350, she then moved to Norway in 1997 to be renamed *Lonnoy* H-38-B.

Silver Harvest BF378. Built by Maaskant Shipyard in Holland as the *Ennie en Appie* in 1968, she came to Scotland in 1979, initially fishing for mackerel with mid-water trawls after being lengthened by 15ft, before pair trawling for whitefish.

The sad sight of three boats being butchered at Inverness. Little more can be said.

Bountiful BF79, an easily recognised Forbes-built boat, completed in 1977, later renamed *Morning Dawn*. The elevated position of the wheelhouse makes it easy to blend in the top deck of the subsequently fitted shelterdeck. Taken as she arrives at Fraserburgh, with wicker herring baskets on the deck, a thing never seen now. One of the crew at the stern is attending to his coiffeur before coming alongside!

Karmarra A571, leaving Aberdeen with the residue of a gale. One of the popular Mk II Spinningdale pocket trawlers, she was built by John Lewis at Aberdeen in 1974 as the *Bevlyn Dawn*. The seiner was later renamed *Donwood* and continued to fish from Aberdeen until being renamed *Karmarra* under a Fife skipper and taking the registration number KY20.

Serene PD 58. I could not resist this shot of the *Serene* arriving at Peterhead on a bright breezy day in November 1980. She was built at Fraserburgh in 1974.

Heritage (I) BF443. The new *Heritage* in June 1967 at Macduff. Built by John Watt at Macduff in the same year, she was the first new purser built in the UK fleet. She also went pair trawling with the first *Prowess* BF460. She was renamed *Herald* BF443 on arrival of the new *Heritage* BF150 in 1972, then *Steadfast* BF443 in 1972, *Shannon* FR293 in 1980, *Pre-Eminent* FR293 in 1985, and *Flowing Stream* PD888 in 1996. Ceasing fishing in 1998, she was used as a cargo boat to freight materials to Sanday.

Gratitude LK173. Built by Irvin's at Peterhead in 1965 as a traditional herring drifter/seiner for Burra Isle owners, she was latterly operated as a seiner and trawler and later fished for prawns. She was fitted with a GRP whaleback during the late 1970s, before being sold to Peterhead in 1980, taking the number PD202.

Angus Rose III ME19. Built for a local skipper from Ferryden, this 49ft 10in overall boat is shown entering Montrose rigged for trawling. Equipped for seining, she was fitted with a seine trawl winch and Beccles warp coiler. She had a stern gantry built by Andrew Galloway of Girvan, possibly the second only to be fitted on east coast boats.

Ability BF9. Built as *Kingsdale* A437 by John Lewis at Aberdeen in 1973, she later became PD359 under the same name. In 1992 as *Kingsdale* she was holed after striking rocks at Kyle of Lochalsh but was re-floated and then completely rebuilt on her original hull in Macduff Shipyard.

Carvida FR347. Unmistakable as one of the big powerful Forbes boats, at 88ft long, this seiner was one of the biggest built at the yard. With the delivery of the new steel *Carvida* FR457 from Millers' in 1989, she was renamed *Ocean Dawn* with the same number. Moving to Peterhead, she was renamed *Pleiades* PD170 and continued seine netting until she was decommissioned in 2002.

Five Sisters OB353. Built by James Noble at Fraserburgh in 1973 as *Valiant II* FR117, her many changes of name included OB353 in 1979, *Aurora* CY463, *Primrose* FR238, then TT233, CY793 and *Supreme* HL1073.

Maid of Honour WK30. She replaced the first of this name which was built in 1950 by David Howarth at Scalloway for a Lybister skipper. This 58.85ft overall boat was built by Mackay of Arbroath in 1980, and was top Wick boat for many years until overtaken by the *Boy Andrew.*

Hawthorn FR25. Built by Tommy Summers in 1953 as the drifter seiner *Ritchies* FR25, which was typical of the shapely boats built at their yard, she was operated by three partners, Tommy being responsible for the design of the boats.

Evening Star LK87. Seen on trials, she was one of the few cruiser-sterned boats still being built in the 1980s, being built in 1981 by the Macduff Shipyard. Built to replace an earlier Miller-built boat of same name, she was renamed *Radiant Star* after being sold to another Shetland skipper. These later boats favoured a much fuller and roomier cruiser stern than the more dainty versions on the earlier boats.

Antaries BF27 and *Pleiades* BF155 These two sister boats were completed by Buckie Shipyard in 2001 with the hulls fabricated by JSC Bars, St Petersburg, Russia, delivered to Invergordon by container ship and towed to Buckie for finishing. They were to a new 16.7ft design by Macduff Ship Design Ltd, the *Antaries* being for John Hepburn to replace the James Noble 1972-built *Silver Gem* and the *Pleiades* for brothers Philip and Garry, who had the original *Alkaid* UL257.

Aquila BA379. This multi-purpose scallop trawler was completed in June 1988 by the Hepworth Shipyard of Paull, a small village on Hedon Haven on the north bank of the Humber Estuary. This was originally a small boat-building yard owned by the Hepworth family but was taken over in 1978 by J.R. Rix & Sons, the Hull-based barge owners and fuel suppliers.

Audacious III BF83. Built by Karstensens at Skagen in Denmark in 1999 as 34m twin-rig trawler fishing mainly off the west coast of Scotland, she was based at Lochinver and Ullapool. Towards the end of 2007 she was sold to Faeroe where she was lengthened. She replaces a previous *Audacious II* which sank off Rockall on 17 January 1998, the six crew being rescued by the Norwegian longliner *Aarsheim Senior*.

Ben Gulvain A751. Built in 1965 by Charles Holmes at Hull, she, along with her sister *Ben Bhrackie* A814, were top fishers, operating off Iceland and then the Barents Sea. In September 1970 she was arrested for poaching in Icelandic waters and fined £7,000. She went ashore north of Aberdeen on 29 January 1976, and, after stripping down, she was refloated and towed to Anstruther where she lay for over a year until sinking at her moorings, eventually being broken up.

Pathfinder OB181. Built with *Ocean Gem* BA265 by Noble at Girvan in 1964 as ringer/trawler BA 252, she was sold as a partner to *Westerlea* OB93, another Noble ringer trawler, and took number OB181. She is possibly one of the last boats to commercially fish with a ring net, and was given a big overhaul in 2006 by Noble's at Girvan, with a new engine and rigged for scallops.

Elizmor BA163 Built as a typical cruiser-sterned 54ft ring netter by James N. Miller at St Monans as long ago as 1948 for Maiden owners as BA343, she was fitted with a seine net winch of the builders' make, and a ring net winch in front of the wheelhouse. At one time she worked ring net pairing in Ireland and took an Irish registration number, being teamed up with *Silver Lining* BA158 for trawling for saithe. She stopped fishing in November 1990 and has been converted to a pleasure boat.

Freedom and *Primrose* at Gairloch. The *Freedom* was built as *Strathyre* by James Noble at Fraserburgh in 1968. The jumble of trawling gear and associated rigging cannot hide her graceful shape.

Prosperity LK428. She was built in 1937 at Macduff, looking a little down at the stern with the weight of the trawl doors and gallows. Her claim to fame was that she appeared in a film about the Loch Ness Monster. Apparently she was built as *Launch Out*, had the number WK235, and was seen, *c.*2006, lying derelict at Avoch.

Faithful Friend and *Silver Cloud II* at Gairloch.

Small yole at Gourdon, still rigged with two masts to suit dipping lugsails. A number of the traditional small fifie and Zulu-sterned boats were still fishing with lines and creels out of Gourdon and Johnshaven.

These boats presented a graceful and characteristic image in contrast to the more bulky modern boats. However, age was catching up by the 1970s, and some were clearly reaching the end of their working lives.

Sharridale AH68 under construction with the hull fully planked at Mackay Shipyard at Arbroath in 1984. This yard was established at the east end of the harbour in 1966.

Arran Venture BA382. The rather tired-looking former 72ft *Venture* LK337 at Troon in August 1990 was considered, in her heyday, a successful herring drift net and seine net boat, based in Shetland. Built by Richard Irvin in 1958 for Burra Isle owners, she won the LHD Trophy twice for herring catches. Following the retiral of her skipper in 1988, she was sold to west coast owners with the same 152bhp Gardner engine and renamed *Arran Venture*.

A view of Buckie with *Grenna Rise*, *Obelisk* and *Brigg*, berthed alongside a so-called 'Mickey Mouse' MMS minesweeper. Herd & MacKenzie built seven of these wooden 105ft vessels and three of the larger 126ft minesweepers between 1941 and 1944.

Brothers FR460. The owners were impressed with the layout on a 110ft stern trawler with sweep winches forward to allow maximum length of net on deck, and had this boat specially designed for them by Napier to be operated by two men on a similar principle on a length of 55ft overall. The reliable Gardner engines were specified, but opted for twin screws due to a limit of 240bhp per engine. Due to capacity constraints in UK yards, early delivery was ensured by the Grofjord yard in Norway. She was later converted to a beamer.

Sirius LK172 with *Radiant Star* LK71 at Hamnavoe Pier at Burra Isle, Shetland. At that time a number of boats lay overnight at the extended pier, built on the old original wooden structure. Built in 1972 in Norway, the *Sirius* as FR127 foundered about fifty-five miles south of Sumburgh Head in January 1994. The crew were airlifted by helicopter. Steaming at high speed to help, the *Rosebay III* PD65 took a lump of water, damaging the deck shelter and flooding the engine room, requiring a pump to be lowered by helicopter.

Day Dawn ME101, *Intrepid* ME68 and *Morning Star* ME106 lying ebbed up at Gourdon. The two inside boats are ex-Admiralty 45ft MFVs; the first is MFV 875, built at Pwllheli, and the second is MFV 991, built at Hull, while the outside boat was built in 1950 by Alexander Noble of Girvan as yard number 10's *Girl Margaret* for a Girvan owner.

The small harbour dries out at low tide, and being exposed to the south-east, mechanically operated protective storm gates can be activated if required.

Research LK62. A picture which graphically illustrates the passing of an era: the forlorn and decaying laid-up Zulu herring drifter *Research* is tied up beside the run-down remains of Shearers' herring station, one of many formerly thriving herring stations along the North Ness in Lerwick. Her final catch of twenty-seven crans in 1968 marked her last season at the herring fishing.

Research LK62 Lying in Hays Dock in Lerwick, the *Research* awaits her fate. Towed to Anstruther, intended for preservation, she lay afloat there for a number of years before eventually being flooded at her berth. Gradually deteriorating, her wheelhouse was removed and, when raised, in the end it was only possible to maintain her structure within a steel cradle. Fortunately, and just in time, her hull was then taken inside to a purpose-built display area within the Scottish Fishery Museum.

Research LK62. The now fragile hull sits on the quay supported within a protective framing, and the characteristic shape of the big Zulu is perfectly illustrated, at once defined by the long raking sternpost and vertical forward stempost. Her sailing ancestry is demonstrated by her graceful underwater shape, deep keel under slack bilges, a fine entrance at the bow and long-drawn-out buttock lines aft.

Avocet FR 162. This 56.78ft overall boat was built by Gerrard Brothers at Arbroath in 1988 and designed by S.C. McAllister & Co. Ltd of Campbeltown, and replaces the skipper's former boat *Blossom.* She is somewhat similar to the earlier Gerrard-built *Radiant Star,* built for local owners and designed to operate twin trawl rigs.

Venturous. This 24.7m wooden boat was built by Jones Buckie Shipyard in 1975 as LK126 for Whalsay owners in Shetland. Moving to the north-east of Scotland under two different skippers in the 1980s, she took the number FR379 before being sold to Castletownbere in Ireland in 1999 and being renamed *Venturous S.*

Enterprise II BF1. Bearing the unique BF number, the *Enterprise II* was the first triple-deck trawler built by Macduff Shipyards, completed in 1999 with the hull fabrication subcontracted to Aveco (Teeside) Ltd. In contrast to other trawlers, she works the trawls off the deck instead of through hatches in the transom.

Ex-*Jaseline* and ex-*Onam*, built at Fairmile Shipyard at Berwick in 1959 as one of the so-called Sputnik trawlers. She is seen here after a major rebuild which involved a complete strip down to the main deck by Macduff Shipyard, renamed *Shamal* BF16.

Sundari PD93. One of the many boats built for Scottish fishermen at Kristensen Yard, Hvide Sande, Denmark, in 1985, to replace an earlier boat lost after springing a leak off Shetland. She had a fully enclosed shelterdeck and was suitable for both seining and trawling, with the trawl warps running from the forward winches through pipes on the deck leading to the gallows blocks. The seine net winch is placed aft of the wheelhouse with the rope reels on the main deck below.

Resplendent PD298. As an 85ft seiner built at Campbeltown in 1979, she was a very successful fisher before being sold and renamed *Fair Morn* INS204 in 1989. In 1996 she was renamed *Oriana* and finally *Utility* FR393 before being decommissioned in 2002.

Dalma BCK113. A section of lying on the shore at Peterhead. It always seems indecent to display the innards of a boat like this. Noticeable is the more rounded bilge, in contrast to the sharper turn of the bilge on most contemporary wooden boats, which would suggest a propensity to roll in a seaway. Originally she operated as an anchor seiner before being converted to a trawler.

Achieve BF223. Designed to fish in deeper waters out to the west of Scotland, as well as in the North Sea, she was completed by Macduff Shipyard in 2001, the third Macduff-built boat for this skipper. With auto trawl twin-rig layout, she has trawl tracks in a central tunnel under the wheelhouse between outboard deckhouses and sweepline winches right forward at the bow.

Green Pastures FR222. Built by Flekkefjord in Norway in 1960 as *Tea*, and then coming to Scotland in 1977 from Sweden, she operated as a herring pair trawler in the season as well as whitefishing. Sold to an Annalong skipper in 1995, she was lengthened and partially shelterdecked, then sold to Plymouth-based owners. She was decommissioned in 2003/2004.

Star Award BF407. Built by Jones at Buckie in 1980, after being bought by an Arbroath skipper in 1987, she had her shelterdeck extended fully aft. In 1997 she moved to Whitby, was converted to twin-rigging and renamed *Star of Hope* FR200. She was sold to Ireland in 2005 and renamed *Cathzelle* B222. She returned to Scotland in 2001 as the *Star of Hope* FR200.

Benaiah BF219 Built by John Lewis in 1975 as *Hesperus*, a design based on the Spinningdale Mk II class, she pair trawled for herring with sisters *Vesper* BF220 and *Lorena* BF227. Later shelterdecked, she was renamed *Benaiah* in 1994 and decommissioned in 2003.

Dorothy Gray A202. Seen in her original guise, and it has to be said not a particularly handsome boat, this 123ft distant-water trawler was built by McTay Marine at Bromborough in 1987. She had a quick-freezing and refrigerated hold as well as frozen catch storage. In 1996 she was bought by Stromness-based owners and completely rebuilt by Richards Dry-dock & Engineering to be suitable for twin trawls and renamed *Norlantean* K508.

Kimara FR176. One of the typical Forbes big boats, the 80ft *Kimara* was built in 1975 and operated as a pelagic pair trawler early in her career, with RSW tanks being subsequently fitted. These were later removed, and she pair trawled and was converted to operate twin-rig trawls latterly. Retaining her original name and number for her whole lifetime, she was broken up in 2002, a few yards from where she was built.

Coronata II BF353. Seen here without her shelterdeck, she was built by the Montrose Shipbuilding Co. Ltd in 1961 as the conventional side trawler *Donside* A552. Subsequent names included *Misty Isle* BA74 and BCK234, *Adastra* BCK234, *Culbean* BCK234 and A55. At times she fished for scallops and pair trawled for herring. She took her final name in 1979 and was decommissioned in 2003.

Sustain PD378. She was a replacement for a previous *Sustain* which was decommissioned in 2003. This new vessel was the former German trawler *Angela* SC26, built by Lubbe Voss in 1986, and underwent a substantial conversion at Peterhead to be suitable for pair seining. She is the third *Sustain* owned by this skipper. The first was PD108, built as *Sparkling Star* by Irvin in 1971, and the next was the *Lupina* PD495, built as the *Morning Dawn* PD195 by J. Hepworth at Paull in 1975.

Adonis LK172 and *Utilise* LK589. The larger boat is on the Prince Olav slipway at Scalloway. Her original cruiser stern was extended by the addition of a transom and towing gantry. The 28ft *Utilise* is a perfect example of the boatbuilders' craft, being built by the Duncan brothers at Hamnavoe in Burra Isle in 1962 and initially used for lobster fishing.

Endurance BF98. Built in Spain by Armon Navia S.A. Spain in 1999, this is another twin-rig trawler. The raking flared bow and prominent bulb with bow thruster is shown prominently in this view on the Fraserburgh slipway.

Fair Morn SY529. One of the shapely Noble-built boats with a sloping top on the wheelhouse, this photograph shows her as a trawler arriving at Lochinver. She was built as *Jasper* SY379 by Alex Noble at Girvan in 1968 as job number 59, then renamed *Santa Maria III* CY38; *Jasper* LN529; *Fair Morn* SY529 and *Fair Morn* BA19.

Strathelliot A446. Built by John Lewis in 1968 as yard number 356 and fitted with a Lister Blackstone ERS6MG/R3 diesel, she was sold to Spain in the 1980s.

Whispering Hope III ME147. Built by John Watt at Banff in 1958 as *Planet* for Shetland owners, she returned south as *Whispering Hope III* in 1992. Early in 1991 she sank after hitting rocks off Oban when coming into the port. Fortunately the crew were able to reach safety. After being raised she was refurbished with a whaleback and had her distinctive sloping wheelhouse raised.

Bonnie Lass III CN126. On the slip at Macduff this rakish-looking boat was built by Gerrard Bros at Arbroath in 1971 as the *Strathgarry* SY88. She then became *Strathgarry* PD91. Moving to Orkney in 1983 and then to Carradale in 1985 when she was renamed *Bonnie Lass III* CN126. Now scalloping, she was renamed after replacing an earlier *Bonnie Lass* CN153 and was sold to Maryport in 2006. In February 1988 she found a bed of clams at Sanda Island and her three-man crew grossed £2,768 for eight hours dredging.

Speyside A4. Built by Richards at Lowestoft in 1978 with sister ship *River Dee*, being a modern class of trawler to replace the former deepwater trawlers. She was later renamed *New Dawn* INS800, and, after a spell laid up, was taken in hand by Buckie Shipyard where she underwent a major transformation which included a fully enclosed stern. Renamed *Jasper* PD174, she replaced the previous *Jasper III* PD174, ex-*Pisces*, built by John Lewis in 1971, which sank in 1999.

Grampian Chieftain A562. With her sister *Grampian City*, she was sold out of Aberdeen in 1990 to the Osprey Fishing Co. of Peterhead, with licences which could be transferred to beamers. Both were built at Goole in 1976, and were 116ft long with 1,700bhp diesels.

Ocean Pioneer FR928. Built in 2000 by Astilleros La Parilla at Gijon in Spain as a twin-rig trawler, featuring a single chine construction instead of a double chine or round bilge, which simplifies fabrication and claims to be only a little inferior in efficiency. The trawl winch is sited forward on the main deck, with warps leading aft over the top of the shelterdeck.

Jasper PD174. Built at Aberdeen in 1971 as *Pisces* A193 in 1971.

Strathgarry PD391. Built by John Lewis at Aberdeen in 1973 as Faeroese *Vest Finnur*, then *Hadegsklettur*, and renamed *Starthgarry* PD391 when brought to Peterhead and shelterdecked, she was converted to a pair trawler in 1973, renamed *Genesis* FR 392, and finally scrapped in 2002.

Monadilath INS140. This was a typically shapely boat by Herd & MacKenzie, completed in 1971 as a ring netter to replace the boat of that name built in 1969 for same owner, which was destroyed by a gas explosion when only a year and a half old. In 1982 she was converted for scallops and fished very successfully until being sold in 2002 to Germany for conversion into a houseboat.

Uberous (2) FR50. Completed in 1973 by Scheeps. De Amstel BV at Ouderkerk, Holland. As *Comrade* FR122 and BA 422 she was a successful purser. A whitefish and pelagic pair trawler from 1982, she was renamed *Uberous* FR50, replacing an earlier boat of this name. She was shelterdecked in 1986, with a new wheelhouse added in 1986, then converted at Macduff in 1988 to a pure twin-rig trawler. She fished until 2005 when she was replaced by the third *Uberous* and made her final journey to the breakers.

Janeen II BCK29. One of the 56ft forward-wheelhouse steel trawlers built by Herd & MacKenzie in 1976. This design was versatile in that they were used for demersal and pelagic trawling. Her original forward whaleback was later augmented by a three-quarter shelterdeck. She was decommissioned and scrapped at Denmark in 2003.

Wanderer A279. Completed by Alexander Noble at Girvan as ship number 56 and registered as BA298 in February 1967, this sturdy 40ft boat had a jaunty appearance and tucked-up cruiser stern typical of her class. She was WK501 for a while, and later took the number A279. When rigged for trawling she was regularly seen on the north-east coast. She was decommissioned in 1993, and broken up at Port Bannatyne on the opposite side of the Clyde from her birthplace.

Nordic Prince BCK18. Decommissioned in 2003, she was built in Norway by Fiskerstrand A/S in 1975 as *Joffre*, later renamed *Sandevaering* and *Suderoy*, before coming to Scotland as *Lestaskjer* in 2000, the only longliner in the fleet. Having been lengthened in 1979, she was fitted with a Mustad autoline system and fished mainly on the west coast and the North Sea.

Celnius II BCK151. A replacement for the earlier *Celnius*, one of the Herd & McKenzie's steel forward-wheelhouse trawlers. Built in 1972 by James N. Miller at St Monans, she was based mainly at Kinlochbervie and fished as far as Rockall. She was lengthened by 5ft and had her stern fully enclosed by Buckie Shipyard in 1997. She was decommissioned in 2002.

Crystal Waters BF209, built originally as *Gem* BCK 213 by G. Thomson & Sons Ltd at Buckie in 1972. Moving to Macduff in1984, she was renamed *Crystal Waters* BF209, fitted with a three-quarter shelterdeck and rigged for twin-rig trawling, operating frequently out of Kinlochbervie and also Fraserburgh for prawns. She was decommissioned in 2002.

Opposite above: Ocean Reward II BCK150, built by Macduff Boatbuilding & Engineering Co. Ltd in 1978 as a seiner trawler, operating on both sides of Scotland. When her skipper bought *Hazelmore III* BCK83 in 1991 she was re-registered as PD50 by her new Peterhead-based owner. Crossing the Irish Channel to Kilkeel in 1996 after being fully shelterdecked, she was renamed *Strathmore* B788. She was broken up on the shore at Kilkeel in 2003.

Opposite below: Brighter Dawn PD62. Seen against the backdrop of Loch Broom, she was one of the many fishing vessels built for Scottish skippers by Sigbjorn Iversen at Flekkefjord. Completed in 1974 as a versatile long-liner, pelagic and whitefish trawler, she also fished for sprats and herring in the Irish Sea. She was decommissioned in 2002.

Brighter Dawn LK47. She came to Shetland in 1954 and fished there until the early 1970s. She is seen here approaching her homeport of Hamnavoe Burra Isle, rigged for seine netting with a winch, coiler and warps laid on the side deck.

Freedom. Built originally as the neat *Strathyre*, she is seen here at Peterhead in what will possibly be her last berth.

Fragrant Cloud II SL PD233. Launched by the Bangor Boatyard in Northern Ireland as B340 for a local skipper as a single boat trawler and herring pair trawler, she moved to Peterhead in 1984 and took the number PD332. She was then renamed *Scotia* with the same number and converted for twin-rig trawling before finally being decommissioned in 2002, to be converted to a cruise boat based at Tongue.

Tyleana BF61. The last cruiser-sterned fishing boat built in Scotland, the *Tyleana* shows the full lines and rounded cruiser stern in its final form. Built at Macduff in 1986, she later took the name *Transcend*.

Dayspring INS 65. It is always a sad sight to see a boat in this condition, here lying at Diabaig in Loch Torridon in the summer of 2006. The feeling is that, no matter how old, some respect should be shown in deference to the safe landfalls despite the many storms and perils encountered. She was built by Herd & MacKenzie in 1958 as *Strathyre* INS65 at their Peterhead yard, and it looks as if her original wheelhouse, which no doubt would have been wooden, has been replaced by steel casing, as seen here.

Dayspring INS65 in happier times entering Macduff Harbour.

Auriga III LH449. This 92ft boat was the last fishing vessel built by Richards Shipbuilders in 1989 at Lowestoft, October 1994, marking the sale of the yard. The final ship built was the ferry *Caledonian Isles* for CalMac, bringing to an end over 100 years of shipbuilding which included numerous fishing boats of all types. She is seen here in the dry-dock at Aberdeen showing her full lines, the bulbous bow being especially prominent.

Vesper INS 453. This Zulu-sterned boat was seen lying outside at Buckie some years ago, thought to be built at Fraserburgh about 100 years earlier. She was later noted lying inside one of Herd & MacKenzie's sheds, it being thought at one time that she would be restored. Of a shape which was common to sailing boats and motorized Zulus of an earlier era, she is in stark contrast to the heavy displacement boats now being built.

Maritan BCK313. The adoption of the transom on trawlers was not universal. However, J. & G. Forbes built the *Constellation*, the 65ft *Kathleen* SY452 and the 66ft *Maritan* FD1. These were followed by *Artemis* FR15 and the bigger *Avenger* BF101. The *Maritan* BCK is seen at Macduff in February 1986, the last boat to use the old cradle on the slipway. At one time she was registered as LH141 before moving to Buckie as BCK313, finally becoming N315 at Kilkeel where she was greatly modernised before being decommissioned in 2002.

Ocean Queen II RO91. Built as far back as 1939 by George Forbes at Peterhead as *Girl Maud* PD100, with a 38bhp National engine, she was later renamed *Marion II* BA184, CN111 and then *Ocean Queen II*. The belt-driven winch, coiler and cabin hatch can be seen on the foredeck.

Ocean Queen II RO91 at work on the Clyde in August 1982, fitted with a trawl winch forward of the original winch. Note the length of her masts.

Resilient PD287. Completed by John Lewis at Aberdeen in 1977 as the yellow-hulled *Glen Artney* A715 after Smith & Hutton (Boatbuilders) Ltd of Anstruther, who subcontracted the hulls to Tees Marine Services Ltd of Middlesborough, went into receivership. Later she was renamed *Resilient* PD287 at Peterhead before going to Orkney as K90 in 1984, and then as FR327 to Fraserburgh, and finally to Ireland before being decommissioned in 2002.

Sealgair A313. Completed by John Lewis in 1971 as an 86ft Spinningdale class trawler with enclosed port side and transom fitted for starboard side fishing, and sister ship to the *Pisces*. She was later renamed *Chemaris* in 1996, when converted for seining and given a shelterdeck and 600bhp Cat engine. She was decommissioned in 2003.

Ribhinn Donn II SY141, built as a ringer/trawler by Alex Noble at Girvan for a Scalpay skipper. She was possibly the last of the ring net type ever to actually use the ring net. With her engine forward and cabin aft, she had an unusual layout intended to make conditions for the crew more comfortable on the Minch crossings. Sold to North Ireland in 1989, she took the number B140.

Huntress BA93. The typical Noble wheelhouse, as exemplified by the *Westerlea* OB93, built at Girvan as a ringer/trawler, also using a small purse net in 1971 and 1972. In 1973 her owners bought the *Pathfinder* BA252 and successfully paired with her. Sold in August 1979 and renamed *Huntress* BA93, she was the last boat to work from Ayr, being decommissioned in 2002 and broken up at Stranraer.

Amity II PD177. Built by Strandby Skibsvert at Denmark in 1989, this boat has been the subject of the enthralling TV series *Trawlermen*. Albeit somewhat dramatised, it is possibly the first realistic depiction of the hazards and complexities of the modern-day fishing boat, the skipper having to balance the conflicting demands of imposed fishing quotas, earning potential, and the overriding need to ensure the safety of the crew and the vessel.

Bervie Braes A414: one of the twenty-two so called 'Sputnik' trawlers built at Berwick by the Fairmile Shipyard as yard number 518 in 1960. As one of the Fair Isle class pocket trawlers, they were termed Sputniks after the Russian satellite at the time. With her sister *Karen* A416, she was built for W.J. Fishing Co. of Aberdeen. The *Bervie Braes* was later PZ253 and then FD23, the open and exposed deck of that era contrasting with the modern fishing boats of today.

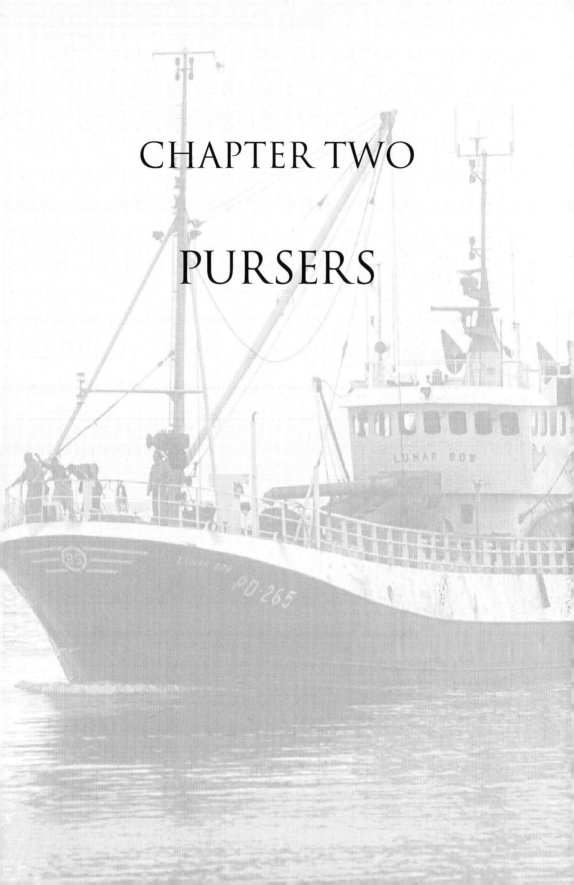

CHAPTER TWO

PURSERS

These are arguably the most impressive vessels in the UK fleet, and are predominantly based at Fraserburgh, Peterhead and Shetland. Of a size overshadowing any other fishing boats, and installed with power hitherto the province of ocean-going cargo ships, their earning potential and corresponding restricted scope of fisheries is exemplified by the length of time they are seen tied up in these ports. In saying that, they have to accept a comparatively nomadic mode of operation to make the most of the allowed quotas of a variety of species.

The design and arrangement of these purse trawlers continues to evolve, with increased speed and the quality of the catch being given special attention. The use of the purse seine net has now been almost completely superseded by the trawl.

Whereas in the past pursers were often lengthened and considerably modified by adding shelterdecks and raising the wheelhouse and so on to meet the changes in patterns of fishing, the trend now is to replace old with new boats, with only a few exceptions which have involved an additional section being inserted.

Ocean Quest BF77. A far cry from the sailing Fifies, Zulus and herring drifters of a bygone age, this close-up shows the impressive curve of the fore end and bulbous bow of the modern purser trawler. She was completed by Astilleros Zamakona SA at Santuce in Spain in 2002, with the *Kings Cross* FR380 in the background.

Radiant Star BF77. This photograph shows the former *Research* LK380 in August 1988, prior to being lengthened by 22.96ft the same year. She was completed in 1980 by Eidsvik Skips at Uskedalen in Norway as *Research* (1) LK380, renamed *Radiant Star* (2) in 1987, *Heritage* (3) BF150 in 1994, *Melanta* in 1996, *Heritage IV* BF150 in 1996 and *Krossfjord* (3) BF70 in 1990. When new she took the name of the last Zulu-type boat to fish in Shetland, where her hull shell is now preserved inside the Scottish Fishery Museum at Anstruther.

Research LK62. Another in the long line of vessels named *Research*, this 70m overall mid-water trawler was built by Flekkfjord Slipp & Maskinfabrik at Flekkefjord in Norway in 2003. She is fitted with hydraulically operated stern doors that can be raised to affect a 1m bulwark above the shelterdeck to provide added safety for the crew working in this exposed area and reduce the amount of water entering through the stern opening on to the working deck. Her main engine develops no less than 7,680kW, to give a speed of 18 knots.

Resolute BF50. Completed in 2003, this 64m overall mid-water trawler by West Contractors AS Olensvag in Norway replaced the *Prowess* and *Courage*. The trawl is handled through a single opening in the transom and the split trawl winches are mounted lower down than normal. Accommodation is provided in fifteen single-berth cabins, with a hospital cabin. The 4,063kW diesel gives a speed of 17 knots, with side thrusters forward and aft.

Fertile FR599. Built as a purser and pelagic trawler by Simek at Flekkefjord in 1989 as *Starcrest* PD232 (2) to replace the earlier wooden *Starcrest*, she was bought by the Tait family and renamed *Ocean Surf* FR225 in 1991, then *Fertile* FR599 in 1995. Lengthened by 24.95ft in 1995, she remained in the Fraserburgh fleet until being sold to Ireland in 2002 and renamed *Havilah* N200.

Accord PD90, built in 1970 by K. Hakvoort Scheeps. NV at Monnickendam in Holland, at 86ft overall with an open aft deck, whaleback and forward wheelhouse. She was lengthened by 22.1ft in 1977, and a shelterdeck was added in 1980, transforming her appearance. Initially she operated as a herring pair trawler, mainly on the west coast of Scotland, but also as late as 1973, and she was on the East Anglian herring fishery in 1975. She fished as a purser and shrimp trawler from 1977, but was sold to Namibia in 1983 and re-registered as L652. Later, in February 1977, she moved to Walvis Bay.

Aquarius II FR365, built by Sigbjorn Iversen at Flekkefjord in 1975 as *Vigilant* PD165 (2). Succeeding *Vigilants* kept the same number. She was used for whitefish trawling as well as pelagic fishing. Shelterdecked in 1977, this photograph shows her after being shelterdecked but not lengthened. She was lengthened by 23.9ft in 1986, and the wheelhouse was raised in 1986. Renamed *Aquarius II* FR365 in 1980 and FR907, she was sold to Angola in 2002.

Lunar Bow (2) PD265. Distinctive by virtue of the tumblehome on the shelterdeck, she was built by Simek in 1978. She fished with purse net and trawled for herring, mackerel and sandeels off season. She was lengthened by 19.5ft in 1979 and then had a stern extension of 6.61ft added in 1983. She was sold and renamed *Westward* (I) BF350 in 1996, then sold to Norway in 1997, renamed *Lonnoy* H-38-B.

Westward (I) BF350. This shot of this rakish boat shows more clearly the added length on the stern.

Taits FR229 Built by Mandal Slipp & Mek. Verksted A/S Mandal in 1978, this versatile boat worked at sandeels, blue whiting, purse seine and pair trawling. She was lengthened in 1985 by 26.25ft, and a whaleback and shelterdeck were added in 1986. Renamed *Taits II* in 2001 and replaced by more modern boats, she was sold by the well-known Taits family in 2002, in Norway, and renamed *Leik* R-44-K.

Serene FR491. Built in Norway in 1978 as *Antares* LK491, a pure purse trawler, for a Shetland skipper, she was a step up from the previous 86.70ft *Antares* LK419. She was sold to another Shetland skipper in 1985 and renamed *Serene* LK491. She then moved to Fraserburgh in 1987 and kept her name and number but changed the registration prefix to FR. She was lengthened by 22ft in 1981.

Orcades Warrior GU5199. Built by Hjelmaas Slipp & Mek. Hjelmas in Norway in 1964 as *Kvalsund Senior* M-153-HO. Bought from Norway in 1980 and renamed *Pegwell Dawn* GU5199, in 1983, under Orcadian ownership, she was renamed *Orcades Warrior*. After taking the Hull number H107, she was sold back to Norway in 1989 as a live fish carrier and renamed *Tjalve*, being scrapped in 1994.

Spes Magna N247. Seen at Peterhead, she was completed by Vooruit Scheeps. at Zaandam in Holland in 1976 for Irish owners. Her modifications included being lengthened by 23.65ft in 1979 and again by a 2ft flared bow and raised wheelhouse and shelterdeck in 1983, and a whaleback in 1987. Sold to Scottish owners in 1990 and renamed *Accord* PD90, she was lost off the Aran Islands, Ireland, on 16 February 1994, when she started leaking forward.

Convallaria V BF58. Built in 1974 by Scheeps. De Amstel BV at Ouderkerk a.d. Amstel, she
was possibly the first Scottish boat to have a chilled dry hold. She took some enormous
catches, like one time off Fair Isle when she was almost pulled over due to the weight
of fish, and another off Guernsey when an estimated 1,000 tons of horse mackerel was
trapped in the net. She was shelterdecked and lengthened by 19.3ft in 1978, and again by
14.3ft in 1987 with a new wheelhouse. She was sold and converted to a trawler in 1998 as
Regina Caeli CY58.

Sunbeam (2) FR478. She was built in 1975 as *Abba* UA960 by Kvina Verft A/S Kvinesdal
and Flekkefjord Slip, and then renamed *Gerda Marie* H-32-AV before coming to Scotland
as *Sunbeam* FR478 in 1987. She switched between purse seining and pair trawling for
mackerel and blue whiting. When photographed she was still carrying her dory under
davits on the port side. She was renamed *Sunbeam II* in 1999 to make way for a new vessel
of same name.

Prowess BF720, built as *Paula* SO720 as a trawler for Irish skipper by Tille Scheeps. BV at Kootstertille in 1980. After being laid up as *Avril*, she came to Scotland in 1994 and was renamed *Prowess*, being converted to a purse trawler, having been lengthened by 39.04ft and a whaleback added to the shelterdeck in 1985.

Paragon PD290, completed by Mandal Slipp & Mek. Verksted A/S at Mandal in 1969 as *Serene* LK297 as a purser. Sold in 1987 without a purse licence, she became a pair trawler. Earlier in her career she ran aground in fog at Lunna on Yell, and in 1994 sank at her moorings in Loch Broom. After being raised, she was towed from Fraserburgh to Dundee where a number of projected conversions fell through, and was eventually broken up there in 1998. She took the name *Sunbeam* (I) FR487 in 1985 and *Paragon* PD290 in 1987.

Omega FD221. Built as the stern trawler *Collena* FD221 by Richard Dunston (Hessle) Ltd at Hessle in 1973. In 1979 she was converted to a purse seiner/trawler and renamed *Glen Rushen*. She was completely transformed in 1987 at a cost of £1.5 million; lengthened by a total of 40.55ft added amidships and aft, she took the appearance of a conventional purser when the new wheelhouse was moved aft, albeit her new engine and some accommodation was still forward, and renamed *Omega*. In 1998 she was sold to Sweden and renamed *Sunnano* GG912.

Linarolynn FR362. Laid down by George Brown (Marine) Ltd at Greenock, she was completed by Forbes of Sandhaven in 1977 as *Coronella* (I) BF277 after the intended outfitters Smith & Hutton of Anstruther experienced difficulties. Lengthened by 19.25ft and shelterdecked in 1980 and renamed *Linarolynn* FR362, *Diligent* FR362 in 1986 and PD314, after a major engine failure she was finally disposed of to Sweden in 1999 and renamed *Hallo* LL139, being rebuilt for further use.

Diligent PD314 in her final years in Scotland.

Challenge (I) FR77. Built by Sigbjorn Iversen in 1971, at only 86.9ft long she was lengthened twice, firstly by 20ft in 1974, as seen here, and then by 24ft in 1987. This latter increase was carried out with sections amidships and at the stern. Also fitted was a new raised wheelhouse. She was renamed *Ocean Star* FR894 in 1996 and *Sparkling Star* (2) PD137 in 2000.

Sparkling Star (2) PD137 after her final lengthening and conversion.

Peter Scott H519. She was originally a side trawler launched as *Cap Bojador* B2491 in 1949 by Société Anonyme Des Anciens Chantiers a Dubigeon at Nantes. Sold to Norway in 1966, she was converted for purse seining. When bought by Hull owners in 1979 she was renamed *Peter Scott*. She was a successful boat based on the Humber, finally being sold to Chilean owners in April 1985. She caught on fire in 1989, but, after being towed back to Talcahauno, was declared a constructive total loss by the insurers, her hull ending up as a floating pontoon.

Quantus (I) N334, built for purse seining and trawling by Voldnes Skib. A/S Fosnavaag Norway in 1979 and operated under a number of skippers. She had a lucky escape in 1988 when, unmanned, she dragged her anchor in Loch Broom. Crew from the *Genesis* N338 went aboard and started her engine to move her clear of the shore. She then went to tow clear the *Convallaria* V BF58, which had gone ashore. She was lengthened in 1994 by 22.96ft and a whaleback was added to the shelterdeck in 1986, before being sold to Iceland in 1996.

    Quantus (I) N334 1979–89; *Quantus* (I) PD379 1989-96; *Ellidi* GK445 1996-.

Starcrest PD232. Considered to be the most successful of all the pursers, she was built in 1972 by Vaagland Baatbyggeri A/S in Norway as *Quo Vadis DM* A778. She was sold in 1978 to a Peterhead skipper and renamed *Starcrest* to replace a pair trawler, PD114, of same name. Shelterdecked in 1983, she passed to St Vincent and Grenadines owners in the Caribbean in 1989 and later the same year to a Cape Town fishing company, taking the number SH1364 but retaining the name *Starcrest*.

Heritage (2) BF150. Originally built at 87.20ft overall in 1972 by Vooruit Coop Ver Scheeps. Zaandam Holland, she was lengthened by 14.57ft and shelterdecked in 1977, and by 23.23ft with a new wheelhouse added in 1984, and finally in 1988 an 8.13ft extension was added to her stern. Operating as a purser and as a whitefish and pelagic pair trawl, with helper boats, she was renamed *Ambassador* (2) BF450 in 1994 to make way for a new *Heritage*. She was renamed *Della Strada* CY158 in 1995, and, after conversion, worked as a trawler.

Kings Cross (I) FR381. Built by Volda Mek. Verk. at Volda Norway in 1975 as *Kings Cross* M-81-HO, she came to Scotland as a purser trawler in 1979. In this shot in Loch Broom she still carries a lifeboat under davits, with another heavier davit to handle a dory boat. She was lengthened amidships and aft by a total of 41.02ft in 1986, and a whaleback was put on top of her shelterdeck. She was sold to a Shetland skipper and renamed *Research* (2) LK381 in 1987, and finally went to Faeroe in 1996, where she was renamed *Saksaberg* TG381.

Orcades Viking K616 Built by Cubow Ltd at Woolwich in 1976 as the *Sedulous* (I) FR228, her length of 89.75ft restricted her carrying capacity to about 133 tons. Renamed *Orcades Viking* (I) in 1979, she was lengthened by 20.75ft in 1980 with a shelterdeck added. Replaced by the much bigger *Orcades Viking* (II) K175, she was sold to Cape Town in 1985 and renamed *Oceana Viking* CTA126, then, in the same year, *Oceana*, and *Oceana Viking* SH14 in 1995.

Pathfinder BA188. Replacing ring netters, she was built by Kystvaagen Slipp & Batbyggeri A/S at Friel in Norway in 1973. She initially pursed and pair trawled in the Firth of Clyde, and was shelterdecked in 1978. After her sale in 1988, she was converted to whitefish trawling and renamed *Prosperity* LH445. Further sale saw her as *Scorpion* PD515 in 1991 and *Resolution* in 1994, before being decommissioned in 2002.

Pathway (2) PD165. Another purser/trawler from Simek in 1984 sold to the Buchan family in Peterhead, designed also as a whitefish catcher. To make way for new boats she was sold and renamed *Unity* (3) FR165 in 1995, and in turn was sold to Norway in 2001 to make way for the *Torbas* (2) F-7-M.

Ocean Way PD465. Built in 1989 by Simek at Flekkefjord as *Ocean Way*, she is seen here in Buchan colours before being sold to Norway in 1997 and renamed *Torbas* (2) F-7-M, before being returned to Scotland in 2001 renamed *Unity* (4) FR165.

Morning Star PD122. Ordered as a seiner trawler in 1973 from Berwick Shipyard Ltd, she was completed in 1976, also with capacity for pursing. When the builders had financial problems she was completed at Peterhead. Due to her small size as a purser, she was converted to a trawler in 1987. Sold to Fraserburgh in 1992, she took the number FR242, then went to Finland in 1997 as FIN194U, and finally back in Scotland in 1999 as *Mariama K* FR242, before being laid up in 2002 after an unsuccessful spell fishing in West Africa.

Torsver FR336, completed in 1966 by Verolme Scheeps. Heusden NV in Holland, a yard better known for the construction of large merchant ships. Originally registered at Bergen as H-65-A, she came to Scotland in 1979, having been lengthened by 14.52ft in 1968. She was shelterdecked and had her wheelhouse raised in 1974. She was sold in 1983 to the Dutch Antilles and then renamed *Chacabuco III* CB2806 in 1984.

CHAPTER THREE

SMALLER FISHING BOATS

Given the uncertainty caused by certain European directives – some examples being the cost of acquiring quotas, capacity limits, limits on days at sea, ever increasing fuel costs and paperwork – many fishermen have opted to operate smaller inshore boats, often miniatures of their bigger sisters as regards gear and outfit, rigged to fish for a wide selection of species such as crabs, lobsters and scallops and so on. Many of these boats are designed to be flexible in that they can be converted to a variety of rigs to take advantage of market trends or fishing seasons.

A measure of the sophistication of these boats, gear and fish-handling arrangements is attested by the fact that many are operated single-handedly. Comparatively large horsepower and consequent high speeds allow them to range over a wide area of operation, and given their comparatively small size this is an advantage in that they have the ability to reach shelter quickly.

Sadly this trend has possibly been reflected in the number of fatalities recorded in this class of boat. Not subject to as high a degree of regulation and survey as the bigger boats, there have been examples of some older boats, never designed as such, being overloaded with winches, net drums and gantries, all of which have reduced their freeboard to dangerous limits with the associated reduction in stability.

Alma LK678. The immaculate *Alma* was built in 1965 by the highly regarded boatbuilders Walter & Philip Duncan of Hamnavoe Burra Isle in Shetland. The perfect line of each plank of the clinker shows off the sweet lines of her hull. She was sold to Loch Fyne in 2007. After a three-year apprenticeship at Hay & Co. at Scalloway, Walter senior started his own business in 1878, building a boatshed in 1892. He built about a dozen traditional Shetland-modelled double-ended clinker types for the Norwegian forces during the Second World War.

Wings of the Morning LK440. A tight squeeze as she is being taken out of the builders' shed, she was the first boat built in 1973 at Scrabster by the Ferro Cement Boatyard as a trawler and scalloper for a Shetland skipper, followed by three of similar size. She is 12.28m overall and moved to Orkney in 1974. The blue-painted boat is now used as a crabber. Unfortunately she went ashore at the south end of Papa Westray in December 2007 and gradually broke up.

Boy Gordon IV A441. Originally a gill netter, she has fished out of Aberdeen with a variety of rigs, including trawling and potting. Building initially started at Montrose Marine in 1989, but when the company went into receivership she was taken to nearby Gourdon for completion by local contractors and helped by the crew. Her hull was built using flexible GRP sheet 'planks' on a wooden framework.

Chloe May FR983, fitted out by Seaway Marine at Macduff on a Cygnus Marine GM 33-type bare hull in 2006, for single-handed potting or mackerel handlining. Fitted with vivier crab tanks and a two-berth cabin, she is noticeable in that no whaleback is fitted forward. Her solid construction and heavy displacement results in a weight of 18 tons.

Trust: a small yole built on Fifie lines, a shape that always appeals. With the move away from sail and the advent of the inboard engine, the trend was to increase the volume of the stern sections to compensate for the increased weight and drag when under power, with the result that the rounded sections aft tapered to a fine entrance forward on the waterline, which was belied by the balanced deck outline hiding the subtle flare of the forward sections.

Queline K1138. Built as *Lauranne* P GU120 by Aqua Star at Guernsey in 1983, later taking the number W250, this hefty GRP construction boat is now owned and operated in Orkney as a potter.

Diligent FR772, a Kingfisher K33 fitted out by the Seaway Group at Macduff, rigged as a crabber with a creel handling roller and winch davit on the starboard side aft of the wheelhouse, and a shooting door on the port side of the transom.

Dalwhinnie A913. Based on a Cleopatra Fisherman GRP boat, she is intended for potting, and operates out of Stonehaven. Completed by Trefjar in Iceland in 2002, she has an additional transom extension which gives a length of 10.1m, to exceed the under 10m limit. She has the well-proven arrangement of duplicate control stations, with a pot hauler and roller on the rail adjacent to a baiting and clearing platform. Crabs are fed via two hatches to two storage bins, and unloading is done via a large central hatch.

Inshallah BRD260. A Norway-built GRP Viksund 42ft boat, this one was bought by a skipper living in Skye. A number of these were imported at around £79,000. Seen here off Aberdeen on 15 July 1980, after her arrival, she was designed to fish with long line, creels, gill nets and rippers. Possibly not entirely successful, she was later laid up for a while and then moved back to Norway.

Iona FR937. Another hull fitted out by Seaway Marine, this is a Kingfisher K26, one of the many potters operating out of Fraserburgh.

Elizabeth BK168, of a design very common among northern boatbuilders, in this case Mathieson of Scarfskerry in Caithness. She still retains her Orkney number after a number of years based at Fraserburgh.

Breadwinner ME66. One of the typical good-looking small boats built by Miller at St Monans, on the style of a Fifie but with much fuller ends, being primarily for motor use. *Guiding Star* is in the background.

CHAPTER FOUR

VISITORS IN
SCOTTISH WATERS

With the loss of the distant-water trawler fishing grounds, it was inevitable that many of the English fishing vessels previously based in such ports as Grimsby and Hull, for example, would have to try and take advantage of the various fishing opportunities in Scottish waters. Some of these deep-sea trawlers were converted or adapted to fish with purse nets or trawls, and were a familiar sight at Ullapool during the Minch mackerel season.

In the 1970s a number of the Ross 'Bird-class' mid-water trawlers were also based at Aberdeen, operating under the BUT umbrella.

Farnella H135. Built by Appledore Shipbuilders at Bideford in 1999 for J. Marr (Fishing) Ltd of Hull as a single boat trawler, this was the largest whitefish vessel to enter the UK fleet that year.

Opposite above: Arctic Raider H440. Built by Stocznia Im Komuny Paraskiej, this rakish-looking stern trawler arrived at Hull on 23 December 1968, having been launched on 31 July the same year. She was built for Boyd Line of Hull, a company founded in 1936. Outward bound for Spitzbergen, from Hull, on 3 December 1975, she had the melancholy honour of being the last trawler to leave the empty St Andrew's Dock.

Opposite below: Arctic Corsair H320. This Boyd Line side trawler was built by Cook Welton & Gemmel at Beverley in 1960, and was the last deep-sea side trawler to operate from Hull. She had to be beached at Sinclair Bay in Sutherland to avoid sinking after colliding with the coaster *Olive* on 14 September 1967. She was converted to pelagic fishing in February 1978, as seen here in September 1979. She was converted back to a conventional trawler in 1985. Her registration closed in January 1988, and she was renamed *Arctic Cavalier* so that her old name could go to a new vessel. After being sold to Hull City Council, she was opened to the public as a museum ship in 1999 under her original name.

Arab H238. Launched on 15 October 1970 by Brooke Marine at Lowestoft as *Ranger Cadmus*, she was the first of a 'C' class quartet of factory freezer stern trawlers for Newington Trawlers. Originally based at North Shields as SN15, when she became part of the BUT fleet, she moved to Hull and was renamed *Arab* (2) H293. After an engine breakdown she was towed to southern Norway by the *Dane* H114, then brought home by a Norwegian tug, sold to Norway in August 1981 and subsequently renamed NY *Pero* M-91-VD, *Pero, Olympic Prawn* and *Kappin*.

Opposite above: Thornella (3) H96. Completed in 1988 by Cochrane Shipbuilders Ltd at Selby in 1988 for J. Marr (Fishing) Ltd, she was the first new trawler to be built for Marr in twelve years, and was followed by her sister *Lancella* H98 in the same year. With the demise of the Hull-based distant water fleet and changing patterns of fishing, most of their landings were at other ports in the UK and on the Continent. The *Thornella* was broken up in 2004 at New Holland on the Humber.

Oppositre below: Swanella (3) H421. This freezer stern trawler was completed by the Goole Shipbuilding & Repair Co. Ltd in January 1967, and in 1969 was Marr's top trawler. She also took part in mackerel fishing, as shown by her presence at Kyle in October 1980. She was sold out of the fleet on 12 June 1981 to Kaare Misje & Co. of Bergen for conversion to a diving support ship, and renamed *Archimedes*. She was renamed *Drive Performer* in 1985, 1988 as *North Sea Commander*, 1990 as *Seaway Commander* and 2004 as *Allied Commander*.

Ross Kittewake GY678. Completed in December 1981 at Selby, she was one of the ten smaller BIRD class under BUT ownership. She fished from Aberdeen in the 1970s. Seven were converted for rig standby duties. Renamed *Desirade*, she was stripped for spares in September 1991 and left Lowestoft for scrapping.

Norfolk Yeoman LT137. Richards Shipbuilders at Lowestoft built a series of steel drifter trawlers which operated in a variety of roles. The *Norfolk Yeoman*, built in 1955, was 86ft 8in long, here seen rigged as a herring drifter. Owned by Small & Co. (Lowestoft) Ltd, she landed 138 crans boxed and another 48.5 crans in her nets on 7 November 1963, to take the herring Prunier Trophy. She was sold in 1968 to Italian owners and renamed *Eros I*, then *Eros Primo* in 1973.

Defiance GY1377. Launched by John Lewis at Aberdeen on 25 June 1966 for Associated Fisheries, this freezer stern trawler was not delivered until 22 November, but, due to engine problems after three trials in two months, she had to go to Immingham for repairs. A top fisher, she gained the Dolphin Bowl on three occasions. She was transferred to Hull as part of the BUT fleet in 1969, and sold for North Sea standby work in 1985, later being renamed *Seaquest Defiance*.

Amarna (3) FD322. Completed in 1976 by the Drypool Dock & Engineering Co. Ltd at Hull for J. Marr, she was the first trawler to gross over £1 million for her twenty-two trips in 320 days at sea in one calendar year, when fishing in home waters. She was sold in 1994 to Donegal in Eire.

Arctic Riever GN23 is a stern trawler, completed in July 1976 by Clelands Ship. Bldg. Co. Ltd at Wallsend for Boyd Line Ltd. Her GN registry is indicative of her management by Wm. Liston Ltd of Granton.

Binks GY617. Built by Herd & MacKenzie at their Peterhead Yard in 1960 as a seiner/trawler for Grimsby owners, she was scrapped in 1996.

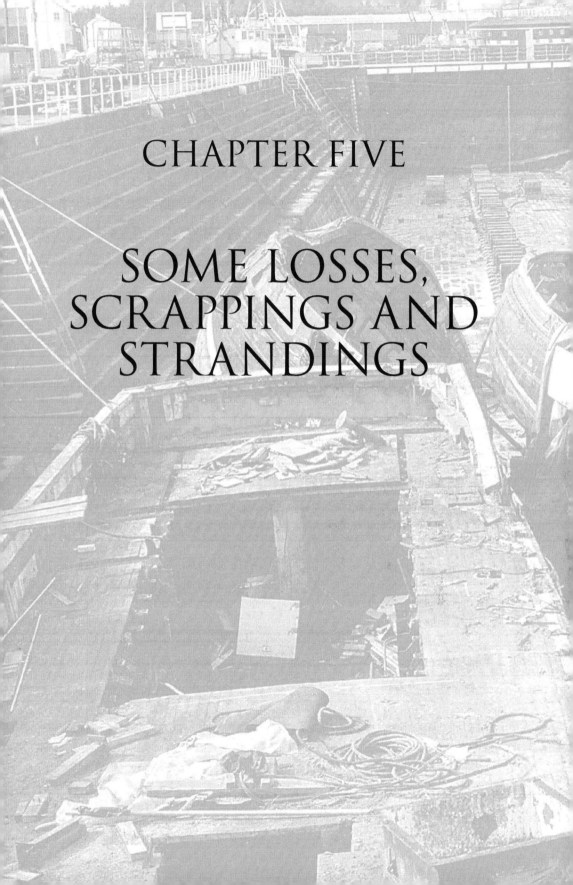

CHAPTER FIVE

SOME LOSSES, SCRAPPINGS AND STRANDINGS

Even with modern well-built boats, the dangers posed by the weather and sea can still exert their toll on lives, as shown by the loss of a number of vessels in the past few years.

It has been claimed that the increased pressure exerted by restrictions in quotas and fishing opportunities, allied to increased operating expenses, has driven skippers to fish in weather conditions at the cost of prudence. Sadly, in the case of boats lost due to rough weather, this has often been accompanied by a major loss of life; boats being suddenly overwhelmed, precluding any chance of rescue.

Apart from stranding, many losses have been due to a failure of the inboard sea connections, often inaccessible under engine room plates, the gradual influx of water going unnoticed until reaching dangerous levels which, in some cases, has been unable to be stemmed resulting in foundering.

Furthermore, the enactment of some of the more controversial aspects of the Common Fishery Policies has seen the scrapping of many otherwise sound fishing boats at home and abroad.

Artemis FR15. Built by J. & G. Forbes of Sandhaven in 1968 as a stern trawler/seiner, she went aground on 2 September 1974 in dense fog on rocks at Sunnyside beach between Logie Head and Findlater Castle. The crew of five gained the shore in their dinghy, and walked to Cullen. The hull broke up soon afterwards. The Kelvin engine was salved and fitted in puffer *Pibroch*.

Angela PD 400. Built by Arma Marine, Brightlingsea, in 1981, she was lost on 6 February 2000 about seventy-eight miles east-north-east of Peterhead. The subsequent MCA report deduced that the cause of the foundering was due to flooding in the deck shelter. Concerns have been raised in respect of the possibility of water being trapped within the confines of a deck shelter if the requisite freeing ports to clear the deck of seawater are inoperable for any reason.

Sharridale AH68. Completed by Mackay Shipbuilders at Arbroath in 1984, she was lost off Peterhead after being run down by the offshore vessel *Huntetor* on 26 February 1995 with the loss of one crewman.

Crimond II KY 246. Built at Fraserburgh in 1973, she capsized and foundered at about 06.30 on 24 April 2001, as result of flooding, possibly the result of a failure in the pipework in the engine room. Fortunately the two crew members were rescued by helicopter.

Opposite above: Sapphire PD 285. Built at Appledore by J. Hinks & Son in 1986, this boat was tragically lost in bad weather on 1 October 1997, about twelve miles east-north-east of Peterhead whilst returning to Fraserburgh in company with the *Elegance*, with which she had been pair trawling. Four crew members lost their lives. After considerable pressure from the families of the lost crew, the wreck was lifted after several delays due to bad weather on 14 December 1997 by the heavy lift barge *Tak Lift VII*.

Opposite below: The sad sight of a number of boats in a dry-dock at Dundee. They were all herded in and the water pumped out to leave them in a jumbled tangle to be broken up where they lay.

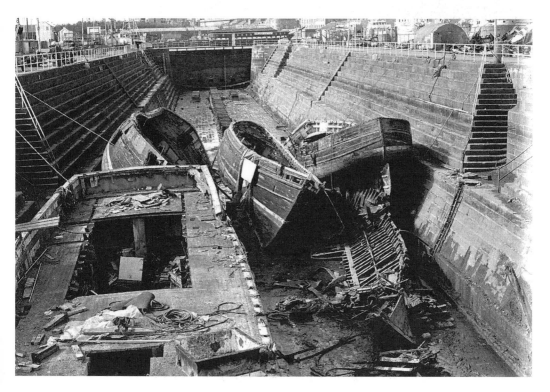

Volente BF262. Completed in 1973 at Fraserburgh, she was rather unusual in that she was propelled by a Baudouin engine. One of a number of boats broken up at Dundee, she has had the deck opened up to remove her engine.

Deeside BF374. Built at Aberdeen in 1972 as *W.R. Deeside*, she was later named *Strathgarry* PD91, *Bairds* PD91 and *Golden Promise* PD91. She was scrapped in 2003.

Annwood A247, built by John Lewis in 1974 as ship number 387. Later she became *Annwood* BF380, then *Sovereign* BF380. She was wrecked after going ashore close to Cairnbulg Beacon on 18 December 2006 when approaching Fraserburgh from an oil standby job, and was not able to be salvaged. Her robust construction is confirmed by the fact that the wreck had still not broken up a year later.

Ross Khartoum. Whilst engaged on oil rig standby duties, she ran ashore on a sandy beach eight miles north of Aberdeen on 19 December 1981 when her engine broke down. With the vessel sitting upright, all the crew were able to get off safely, but being well up on the beach she could not be re-floated and was broken up.

Sheriffmuir. Another standby former trawler, she went ashore in dense fog three miles north of Aberdeen at 05.00 on 1 October 1976. A breeches buoy was soon deployed, but being in no danger the six crew members opted to wait until low water, when they climbed down a ladder into a trailer towed by a tractor. The wreck was broken up in situ.

Coastal Emperor. On 6 December 1978 in a force 7-8 south-south-east gale, the former trawler, now used on oil rig standby duties, ran ashore 1.5 miles north of the River Don. As she was on an even keel and in no immediate danger, the crew were taken off by breeches buoy next day. After several unsuccessful attempts to haul her off, she was abandoned in March of the next year, being broken up where she lay.